Mimesis

Mimesis:
On Appearing and Being

Samuel IJsseling

translated by Hester IJsseling and Jeffrey Bloechl

Kok Pharos Publishing House

Originally published as *Mimesis: Over Schijn en Zijn*,
© Ambo, Baarn 1990.
Translated by Hester IJsseling and Jeffrey Bloechl
English translation © 1997 Kok Pharos Publishing House
P.O. Box 5016, 8260 GA Kampen, the Netherlands
Cover disign: Geert Hermkens
ISBN 90 390 0273 8
NUGI 611

Contents

I. Mimesis

Since the Pythagoreans, in Plato and Aristotle, and in the whole of the Greek literary and rhetorical tradition, the notion of *mimesis* plays an important role. It is one of the root words by which all sorts of widely divergent phenomena are voiced in European culture. The domain of the mimetic is extensive and interwoven with many other issues. It branches out on all sides and is therefore difficult to determine or delimit. As well, even translating the original Greek term *mimesis* poses considerable difficulties, first because its meaning is not always the same from one author's text to that of another, but also because the meaning is in each case dependent on the domain of phenomena to which it is supposed to apply. The usual Latin translation is *imitatio*, a word which is equally polysemous and, moreover, does not fully comply with what the Greeks have tried to express by the notion of *mimesis*. Among the possible English translations of the Greek *mimesthai* are: to imitate, to follow, to mimic, to ape, to counterfeit, to forge, to reproduce, to copy, to mirror, to double, to depict, to represent, to render, to impersonate, to repeat and to translate, to recite and to cite, etc. Each of these again poses all sorts of new problems. A certain ambiguity is striking in most of them. This ambiguity has to do with the common but not self-evident opposition between the real and the unreal, the authentic and the inauthentic. In any case, the word mimesis can be used in a positive as well as a negative sense. This is clear in relation to imitation, which has an explicitly positive meaning in the expressions *omnis ars imitatio naturae* (Seneca) or *imitatio Christi* (Thomas à Kempis), but which can also point to the fact that we are dealing with the unreal, the not original, the pseudo, a sham or a counterfeit. Instead of ambiguity, then, one might rather speak of polysemy, for the mimetic occurs on many different levels. This polysemy is of the same order as that of appearance (*doxa*) and appearing, making one's appearance and presenting oneself (*phainesthai*), to which the mimetic is essentially linked.

II. Drama and Literature

The notion of mimesis is said to have its origin in the world of music and dance, and then to have later passed into a theory of drama, literature and the visual arts, finally coming into a theory of language, education and culture.[1] In music, certain movements are repeated. A same movement is taken up again in a slightly different way. In and through this repetition something like music comes into being. Every form of rhythm supposes repetition of the same and difference. Besides this repetition of the same movements, motives and measures in a slightly different way, the piece of music as a whole can also be repeated or presented again, even in a different place and under different circumstances. The same can be said of dance and, to a certain extent, of rites and ceremonies. Dance is mimetic, not so much because the dancers represent something – which may also be possible – but more so because of the fact that each dancer imitates the other and every movement supposes and evokes similar movements. Rites and ceremonies are essentially marked by repetition and repeatability. The same acts must be carried out and the same words spoken. Changes in ritual are scarcely tolerated and are usually accompanied by conflict. Music, dance and rites, together with the telling of tales belong

---

1. H. Koller, *Die Mimesis in der Antike. Nachahmung, Darstellung, Ausdruck.* Francke Verlag, Bern 1954.

to the ingredients from which drama, tragedy and comedy may have originated and been built up.

Drama is mimetic in many respects. The actors bring certain personages on stage, where their actions, words and gestures are imitated and represented. In this, the actors usually follow a scenario, a story or a text prescribed by the author, and they speak and act according to the specifications of the author and the director. The acts are not 'really' committed and the dialogues are not 'really' carried out, but everything is played out, or play-acted. It is a matter of the rendering of possible actions and dialogues. Not only do the actors imitate and represent something, but the plot, intrigue or story is also mimetic. A 'whole' of events is produced.[2] Most often, these acts have not really happened, but belong to the possible. In this connection, Aristotle, in a passage from the *Poetics* on story (*epos*) and drama (*drama*), remarks that 'the poet's function is to describe not the thing that has happened, but a kind of thing that might happen, i.e. what is possible as being probable or necessary. The distinction between historian and poet is not in the one writing prose and the other verse – were one to put the work of Herodotus into verse, it would still be a species of history; it consists really in this, that the one describes the thing that has been and the other a kind of thing that might be. Hence poetry is something more philosophic

---

2. ['Produced' translates *opgevoerd*, which simply means 'put on stage', or 'performed'. However, perhaps the English word might here be applied not only in the colloquial sense which repeats the meaning of this Dutch word, but also in its strictly literal sense: to pro-duce is to bring forward, both as in bringing to light and as in giving birth to.]

and of graver import than is history, for its statements are of the nature rather of universals than particulars, whereas those of history are of particulars.'[3] This is said within the broader framework of the problem of mimesis, with which the *Poetics* begin and where the question is raised concerning the essence and the origin of poetry, epic and drama. According to Aristotle, these lie in the fact that it is human nature to imitate and represent others, and in the pleasure that man gets from representing and from the recognition of doing so.[4]

From of old, drama has been glorified as one of the most perfect art forms, but it has also been vilified as black art and trickery. Within living memory, man has been captivated by it, but it has also been experienced as exceedingly threatening. Theater has been looked upon as a mirror in which man sees himself reflected and in which he is revealed to himself, but also as a world of appearance and illusion. For many it functions as a metaphor for human existence and as a model for understanding what it means to be human, but at the same time it is understood as the most unreal. The *fare bella figura* (i.e., to play-act in everyday life), glorified in the Baroque period, is considered by some a refined form of culture, but by others is condemned as contrary to sincerity and nature.[5]

For Plato theater, like mimetic arts in general, is a world of appearance and deception. According to him, the poets and storytellers should be excluded from the

---

3. Aristotle, *Poetics* 1451a 36*ff* [translation according to Bywater].
4. *op. cit.*, 1448b 7-8.
5. Peter Burke, *Anthropology in Early Modern Italy*, Cambridge, UP 1987.

ideal state. They wish to replace reality with words and images and in this way would make the world into a cave.[6] The telling of tales, at least, does receive some of Plato's mercy, in so far as use is made of indirect speech and to that extent that some pedagogical value is conceded them. Philosophy, however, as the seeking after truth, is something different to him. It is the interruption of narrative and the rupture of doxa by the asking for true essence. In his eyes, matters are somewhat worse in the case of actors and the world of the theater. The biggest problem here is that the actors do not speak in their own name, do not mean what they say and therefore do not consider themselves responsible for what they say. When somebody on stage declares his love for someone else, he recites a text that someone else has written for him, he speaks in the name of the character he impersonates, he is not behind what he says, and no consequences may be drawn after the performance. For Plato, such speech is unethical and illegitimate. It is not even speaking, but a pretending, an imitation of real speech, and in fact it, then, has a mimetic relation to real speech.

Plato distinguishes between those people who have the right to speak and those who do not.[7] Only he who speaks in his own name, who is fully behind what he says, who is alive to what he means and who considers himself responsible for his words, only he has a right to speak. All other speaking is illegitimate, ethically objectionable and

---

6. C. Verhoeven, *Het medium van de waarheid. Beschouwingen over Plato's houding tegenover de poezie.* [= The Medium of the Truth. Reflections on Plato's Relation to Poetry] Ambo, Baarn 1988, p. 149.

7. J.-L. Nancy, *Le partage des voix.* Galilee, Paris 1982.

a sham. To the latter also belong every form of declamation, recitation and citation, in other words 'introductory speech', which is one of the many forms of mimesis in Plato.

Owing to this division between those with a legitimate voice and those without one, Plato's dialogues are marked by a certain tension. It will not have escaped the good reader that in many respects these dialogues have a narrative character and that they are even 'dramatic': that is to say, they are of the nature of a play. Gorgias might even have spoken here of a parody.[8] Thus, most of Plato's dialogues begin with the story of Socrates meeting someone by chance, going somewhere with him and beginning a conversation. Plato recounts all manner of things which happen during these conversations. As happens in staging or in literature, he puts words in the mouths of Socrates and his interlocutors – words that they could possibly have said, but in fact did not. In spite of his tirade against literature, Plato is a great literary man. To the 'heroes' of epic and tragedy he, as it were, opposes *his* hero of the truth, namely Socrates, who ultimately pays for his heroism with death. In this way, one story is counterposed to another.[9]

In connection with Plato's ideal of speech, one can ask oneself whether it is ever possible to speak really and fully in one's own name.[10] When people put forth speech, they

---

8. Cf. Gorgias of Leontini, fragment 15 a.
9. One finds this theme in the work of Walter Benjamin and Hannah Arendt, among others. Cf. Ph. Lacoue-Labarthe, *L'imitation des modernes. Typographies II.* Galilee, Paris 1986, pp. 274-275.
10. S. IJsseling, 'Het grote geheugen. Over Plato, de dichters en de sofisten' [= 'The Great Memories. On Plato, the Poets and the Sophists'], in: J. Boonen, et. al., *Gisteren en morgen voorbij.*

use words that are the words of others, frequently citing both implicitly and explicitly, but without full insight into what is given to them. This means that speaking always to a certain extent has a mimetic character. In all speech there is something of a repetition of the words of others. We will return to this. It is not impossible that one of the intentions of Plato's dialogues is the bringing to light of this very problem. In any case, this certainly does show up to a close reading, especially when one keeps one eye to the distinctive rhetoric marking these dialogues. However, what Plato explicitly states concerning speech is another matter. The language of the theater – and this is Plato's example for all sorts of other forms of inauthentic language usage – is the contrary of what real speech is or ought to be. It is, in short, the mere copy, or imitation, of that real speech, mimesis.

A contrasting point of view is taken by the Sophist Gorgias. With respect to tragedy and literature in general, he remarks: 'He that deceives is more honest than he who does not, and the deceived is wiser than the undeceived.'[11] Here, deceiving and being deceived first and foremost have the meaning of moving in the field of *doxa* and *mimesis*, where the Sophists were masters. Gorgias' remark on literature is connected to his conception of the power of the word, the *logos*. *Logos* here means something like discourse, or story. In his *Panegyric on Helen*, which

---

Tweemaal vier opstellen over de oudheid. Peeters, Leuven 1987, pp. 45-55.

11. Gorgias of Leontini, fragment 23 [rather than translate from the German *Reden, Fragmente und Testimonien,* Hamburg 1989, which IJsseling cites, we give directly the English translation from K. Freeman, *Ancilla to the Pre-Socratic Philosophers,* Basil Blackwell, Oxford 1966, p. 136].

is also a panegyric on rhetoric, he says: 'Speech [*Logos*] is a great power which achieves the most divine works by means of the smallest and least visible form.'[12] The word has such great power, he argues, because man possesses neither a commanding view of the entire past, complete insight into the present, nor certain knowledge of the future – in other words, because he stands in time. One of the most wondrous things that the word can bring about is letting people and things appear and occur just as they do appear and occur in fact. In this way, one presentation of things makes Helen appear to us as guilty and the source of great misery, while by another presentation she is innocent and a victim. For Gorgias, the word is in fact not a sign that stands for a pre-given reality or thought, but a means by which something can be brought about and a particular effect achieved.[13]

It is debatable whether in Gorgias one can still inquire after the truth. Plato will contend against him that neither the question of truth nor that of justice are posed. Perhaps Gorgias' view is less suitable for properly posing the question of what science is, but it is in fact more suited than that of Plato to formulating what happens in literature. In whatever way the relation between science (philosophy) and literature may be thought, the history of this relation is governed by a certain interpretation of mimesis.[14]

12. Gorgias of Leontini, fragment 11 [in Freeman, *Ancilla*, p. 132; for what follows, see also fragments 11-14].
13. S. IJsseling, 'Macht, taal en begeerte' [=, 'Power, Language and Desire'] in: *Tijdschrift voor Filosofie* 41(1979), pp. 375-404.
14. J. Derrida, 'La double seance', in *La Dissemination*, Seuil, Paris 1982, pp. 208-209 ['The Double Session' in *Dissemination*, translated by B. Johnson, Athlone Press, London 1993, pp. 173-174].

III. Similarity or Difference

In the metaphysical tradition, the problem of mimesis is cast in the light of the question of truth and the latter is thought as correspondence (*homoiosis, adequatio*).[15] With respect to mimesis, all emphasis is on the question of whether or not the imitation, depiction, impersonation, rendering, reproduction or description, on the one hand, corresponds with the original, example, model, reality, idea or nature, on the other. This correspondence can be more or less perfect and can take on all sorts of shapes, including presentation, representation, transposition, transfiguration, idealization, generalization, composition, perfection, etc. Throughout, the resemblance or correspondence is in the foreground.

This is clearly the case with Plato. The Platonic theory of mimesis coincides with the Platonic conception of truth as correspondence and identity.[16] According to

---

15. [Both here and in the title of this chapter, IJsseling uses the same word, *overeenkomst*, which we have translated in the first instance as 'similarity' in order to remain within more colloquial English, and henceforth as 'correspondence' in an attempt to preserve the intended resonances of these remarks with the related analysis of the problem of truth appearing in Heidegger's 'Vom Wesen der Wahrheit' in *Wegmarken*, Klostermann, Frankfurt a.M. 1967, pp. 73-97 ('The Essence of Truth', trans. J. Sallis, in M. Heidegger, *Basic Writings*, Ed. D.F. Krell. Harper and Row, New York 1977, pp. 117-141).]
16. E. Escoubas, *Imago Mundi. Topologie de l'art*. Galilee, Paris 1986, p. 20.

Plato, the being that exists in reality has a mimetic relation to the idea of which it is, in so far as determined by space and time, an imperfect reflection. Art – the visual arts as well as literature – has a further mimetic relation with respect to reality, of which it is only an imperfect rendering. Thus, the bed made by the carpenter is a shadow of the idea 'bed' and the depicted or described bed is still more removed from the original idea. One can not sleep on it, says Plato, just as one can not satisfy one's hunger with painted or described food.[17] The most perfect rendering of reality would be the mirror, because it is even able to immediately reflect every change and movement. Yet this reflection is also the most unreal. This conception of mimesis supposes a certain hierarchy among beings.[18] What is of interest here is an ever lessening degree of reality, truth and consistency. Further, mimesis in all its different forms adds nothing to either the idea or reality. An absolutely perfect rendering would coincide with the thing rendered, while mimesis brings with it a non-identity or difference.

With Aristotle, things are somewhat different. In the *Poetics* mimesis, here usually translated as 'representation', functions to allow reality to appear (in a new way). The work of art, that is to say the image or the poem, can show the essential and the necessary in the accidental and the transitory. In a certain respect it is therefore higher than reality. In the *Physics*, where there is mention of *mimesis tes physeoos*, Aristotle speaks of the craftsman (e.g., the carpenter, the doctor, the poet) who

17. Plato, *Republic* X, 596 a, b.
18. W.J. Verdenius, *Mimesis. Plato's Doctrine of Artistic Imitation and Its Meaning to Us.* Brill, Leiden 1949.

imitates or follows nature in its working and brings it to completion or perfection with his own work (*epitelei*).[19] Thus, in Aristotle mimesis does in fact add something to reality. It is even possible to interpret Aristotle such that he states that reality as reality can appear only by means of mimesis, more or less in the way in which there can be a question of truth only in the judgment. With this interpretation, we come close to Hegel who, for that matter, was a good reader of Aristotle.

Hegel, who quotes Aristotle several times in his *Lectures on Aesthetics*, argues that the task of art does not lie in being as faithful an imitation of so-called reality as is possible, but that the point is to raise this reality to a higher level, whereby freedom and fantasy, imagination and creativity play an important part. He speaks rather ironically about Zeuxis, a painter from antiquity of whom it was said that he could paint grapes so well that even the pigeons went for them, which was then considered a great artistic triumph. For Hegel, this is not great and true art, but rather something on the order of a feat.[20] According him, art is not about imitation of nature and things, animals and human beings, but a doubling of man and his world, and the recognition of himself and his world in this doubling. The task of art is to disclose the truth and to bring about a reconciliation of the sensuous and the spiritual.[21] Art is understood here as a first

---

19. Aristotle, *Physics* II, 1, 193 a.
20. Hegel, *Vorlesungen über die Ästhethetik I*. Werke in zwanzig Bänden, 13. Suhrkamp, Fankfurt a.M. 1970, p. 66 [*Aesthetics. Lectures on Fine Art*, trans. T.M. Knox, vol I. Clarendon Press, Oxford 1975, pp. 42-43].
21. *ibid.*, p. 82 [*Aesthetics*, pp. 54-55].

moment in the great event of truth that exists in the coming to itself and the being reflected in itself of the whole or the absolute.[22] For Hegel, art is at the service of truth -truth understood, indeed, not simply as correspondence, but as positively coinciding with itself, as identity, be it an identity of the identical and the non-identical.

Trying to solve the problem of mimesis out of phenomenology, more specifically out of the thought of Heidegger, E. Martineau states: 'Mimesis does not reproduce, but inscribes a difference. But how not to be party to this difference?'[23] The author then attempts to understand mimesis not out of identity or correspondence, but difference and distinction.[24] Similar approaches to the problem of mimesis are taken by Gilles Deleuze in his *Difference and Repetition*,[25] Jacques Derrida

---

22. Hegel, *Encyclopedia for the Philosophical Sciences*, paragraphs 556-563.

23. E. Martineau, 'Mimesis dans la *Poétique*: pour une solution phénoménologique', in *Revue de Métaphysique et de Morale* 81(1976), p. 448 [French retained by Professor Ijsseling; translation ours].

24. In many cases I prefer the word 'distinction' to 'difference.' Distinction is that on the basis of which beings are distinguished and distinguishable, in the sense of perceivable. This distinction may not be understood as opposition and is of a different order than the distinguished and distinguishable beings.

25. G. Deleuze, *Différence et répétition*, PUF, Paris 1986 [*Difference and Repetition*, trans. P. Patton. Athlone Press, London 1994]. See also G. Deleuze, *Logique du sens*, Minuit, Paris 1969, especially 'Simulacre et philosophie antique' (on Plato and Lucretius, pp. 292-324 [*The Logic of Sense*, trans. M. Lester and C. Stivale. Athlone Press, London 1990, especially 'The Simulacrum and Ancient Philosophy' pp. 253-279].

in his 'The Double Session',[26] Philippe Lacoue-Labarthe in his *Le sujet de la philosophie. Typographies I* and *L'imitation des modernes. Typographies II*[27] and Eliane Escoubas in her *Imago Mundi*.[28]

Setting forth from difference easily leads to misunderstandings. To be clear, the present concern is not to point out that there is a difference between rendering and the rendered, reproduction and the original or wording and reality. This, of course, would amount to no more than another variant of the act of highlighting correspondence. It would be to emphasize once again the varying degrees of perfection attained by each form of mimesis. Instead, the issue here is a difference between one rendering and another, one reproduction and another. The traditional opposition between original and reproduction is canceled out, or at least takes on new meaning. This does not mean that reproduction now receives priority over the original, as F. Lyotard seems to argue.[29] In that case, one would have to speak of an 'inverted Platonism.' On the contrary, the point here is a difference that is 'older' and 'more original' than the difference between rendering and the rendered – a difference that to a certain extent comes into being with mimesis and that is presupposed in mimesis. It is this difference which makes it possible for something to be distinguished in the sense of being perceived, and for

---

26. J. Derrida, *op. cit.*
27. Ph. Lacoue-Labarthe, *Le sujet de la philosophie. Typographies I.* Galilee, Paris 1979, and *op. cit.* See also S. Agacinski, et. al., *Mimesis des articulations.* Aubier-Flammarion, Paris 1975.
28. E. Escoubas, *op. cit.*
29. Ph. Lacoue-Labarthe, *L'imitation des modernes*, pp. 272-284.

there to be distinctions because of which things are neither the same nor indifferent. This is a 'difference' closely interwoven with time, repetition and repeatability, and the non-simultaneity that is connected with them. What is at stake in the question of such a difference is the essence of truth, the identity and recognizability of beings and the production of meaning.

It is characteristic of mimesis that a displacement takes place. In and through mimesis, reality appears on a different level. This level is neither necessarily a lower one, as Plato thinks, nor a higher one, as Hegel and perhaps also Aristotle think. Human beings and events, things and situations occur and appear in another place and at another moment. They appear on stage, in literature, in a work of art or in any other form of imitation. The displacement which has a spatial as well as a temporal character is possible on the basis of a difference that comes into being in and through mimesis. The possibility to appear in another place at another moment is essential for every form of appearance. Without repetition and repeatability there can be no meaning or sense. Mimesis and appearing or presencing (*doxa*) are closely connected to one another.

IV. Mimetic Relations

In the traditional view of mimesis there is sometimes a tendency to confine mimesis to the domain of the arts – visual art and literature. This occurs especially in the modern age, but much less so in antiquity. For the Greeks and Romans every form of *techne* and *ars* is mimetic, but what they understand by this is certainly not the same as what has been called art since the Renaissance. For them it is the skill of bringing something about or of making something in a competent way. In antiquity, however, it is not only making (*poesis*), but also acting (*praxis*) that is mimetic. Thus, as we have seen, for Plato quoting or, more generally, repeating what others have said and done is mimetic. The art of poetry is mimetic because the poets do not speak in their own name, but are spokesmen of the gods,[30] and sophistry is mimetic because the Sophists move only on the level of appearance and imitation and for that reason are only would-be philosophers, or imitation philosophers.[31] And thus also for Aristotle, who values mimesis in a much more positive way than does Plato, not only poetry and craftsmanship have a mimetic structure, but every learning process as well. One learns by imitating. Furthermore, according to the classical rhetorical tradition, being eloquent, courteous and right-minded is

---

30. Plato, *Io* 354e.
31. E.A. Havelock, *Preface to Plato*, Oxford 1963, pp. 20-35.

learned in the first instance by following the great examples. In the end, as old wisdom would have it, all learning is by much repeating. *Repetitio est mater studiorum.* It is therefore that the domain of mimesis can be said to cover quite a bit more than what since modern times is called art.

If one wishes to properly inquire after what mimesis is, then, as opposed to common practice, one must choose a starting point that is as broad as possible. The mimetic occurs in many domains, and it is probably possible to point out something of the mimetic wherever there is a question of relations. Representations of every kind, such as statues, paintings, drawings, photographs, maps, and emblems bear a mimetic relation to what is represented. The representation neither coincides with the represented nor is necessarily a copy of it. One can restrict oneself to a few remarkable features. An object can be represented, as can a state of affairs, a situation, an event or an act. There are also representations that render something that does not occur in material reality, such as an idea, a thought, a wish, a fantasy or a command. Even representations can be represented, and this can be done in many ways. For instance, they can be reproduced. The representation or reproduction of a representation again has a mimetic relation to this representation. Most representations are in fact representations of representations and, in any case, every representation refers to other representations to which it is committed in its capacity to be a representation. But the particular representation at the same time distinguishes itself from these other representations, and in this way those meanings can be produced that are in fact produced by that representation. Furthermore, it can be stated that every representation is in a certain way produced, though not necessarily by man. An example of this would be a mirror image, which can come about without human interference. In most cases, the produced representation is recognized, and this recognition does seem to be the privilege of man, although this is not entirely certain. On the basis of being produced and recognizable, productive and receptive mimesis are usually distinguished. The two generally go together, but can be distinguished all the same.[32]

What is said here about representation also holds for what is sometimes called impersonation or rendering, for example on stage or in film (both feature film and documentary), and wording or rendering in a novel, a treatise, an account or, more generally, a text. Here too there is a mimetic relation to the rendered. A play or a film can be reproduced, that is: staged and shown again and again for another audience, at another time and even in the same time in another place. Of one and the same text, there may exist many copies. Each text can be multiplied in many different ways and read and reread by many different people. In addition to this, it may be remarked that, on the one hand, each separate perform-ance and each copy is a reproduction of the same play, the same film or the same text, but that, on the other hand and at the same time, it has its own existence and can produce its own meanings. A play, a film and a text always refer to other plays, films and texts, if only because each belongs to a certain genre, adopts a certain

---

32. H.G. Gadamer, *Wahrheit und Methode*, J.C.B. Mohr, Tübingen 1960, pp. 108-115 [*Truth and Method* (no translator given). Sheed and Ward, London 1975, pp. 99-108].

24

thematic and means of elaboration, reacts to other plays, films and texts, and, in order to be produced, requires certain technical and rhetorical skills to be acquired by imitation, a lot of looking and learning, and reading. Moreover, a film can be based on a book and books can be written about films. These are mimetic relations that can scarcely be unravelled.

A play or a film are usually understood, provided that certain conditions are complied with on the part of the play or film, as well as on the part of the spectator. This understanding is a form of recognition. One recognizes oneself and one's fellows, the situations one does or could possibly find oneself in, the conflicts with which one is confronted and, perhaps, the dreams one entertains. Of course, this can also be the case with a story or a novel. Recognition, or receptive mimesis, has a rather intricate structure. Drama, film and literature can function as a mirror which has a revealing effect. Frequently, it is possible to imagine oneself in the position of the characters who appear, and to identify with them. One can even imitate what one has seen and read, and follow what is represented and rendered. Of this latter, a great many eloquent examples can be given.[33] Likewise, a form of recognition also appears in the reading of a scientific treatise, an account, a description or legal text, a user's guide or a catalogue. Without it, a text would not be

---

33. The classical example is Goethe's Werther, who assumes he is completely alone with his grief when in fact he is an imitator. His suicide is followed by others who also take up the entire staging. So, too, with Emma Bovary. Indeed, nearly all of Flaubert's personages are good examples. Most of them are readers whose fate is to a large extent determined by their relation to what they have read.

legible. The text is placed in a greater whole or network of already existing texts and the many references to them are followed to a varying degree. This network of texts and these references are of a different sort in every kind of text so that each particular kind of text therefore requires a particular way of reading. The above also holds, *mutatis mutandis*, for the spoken word, the story told, the given speech or discourse or verbal communication.[34]

Against what is said here, one may object that in the case of scientific treatises, communications, etc., there is no question of mimesis. Such an objection makes sense only if mimesis is confined to the arts, meaning visual arts and literature. In any case, something is rendered even in scientific texts, and rendering is one of the possible translations of mimesis. However, it can be said that the sort of rendering seen in literature is of a different nature than that in science. One task, then, will be to distinguish the different forms of mimesis, but this does not mean that in a scientific text it would not remain a matter of mimetic relations. The opposition between fiction and non-fiction, to which appeal is so often made, is not of much help here. It can be useful in the classification of

---

34. The relation between the spoken and the written word is itself of mimetic nature. This, however, does not mean in any way that the written word is an imitation, a rendering or a perfection of the spoken word. The intricacy of this relation becomes evident in, among other things, the word that is 'spoken' on stage, in the theater, and in the theater that is everyday life. Is this a spoken word or a written word? Which comes first and which follows? An actor repeats what a playwright has written. When we speak in everyday life, do we not often say what is prescribed? In any case, we would speak in a very different way if there would be no writing.

texts, but it does not clarify much. The word fiction, which goes back to the Latin *fingere*, evokes a concatenation of meanings reaching from making, manufacturing, composing, ordering and arranging to imagining, fantasizing, concocting, feigning, pretending and simulating, meanings that all belong to the possibilities of mimesis. Employed in the sense of concoction, and usually in order to oppose literature and science, the term fiction is an extremely problematic interpretation of the mimetic which is determined by a specific kind of metaphysics. The problem of the relation between science and literature and the confusion that is caused by it, is closely connected to the history of this interpretation. The opposition between fiction and non-fiction is one of the moments of that history.[35]

The mimetic is not restricted to the representation, or rendering, and the recognition of it. There is also the entire domain of imitating and copying. We have already alluded to this when we spoke about reproduction. Things can be imitated. Thus, to reprise (to cite and to imitate) Plato's example, one can imitate a bed that is still a bed and not an imitation bed. However, one can also imitate something, for example a diamond, where it is in fact a question of an imitation or paste-diamond. Countless things in our technical world are fabricated in large quantities looking perfectly alike and are similar in everything except for the difference of place which is their only distinguishing feature. In addition, all kinds of synthetic materials, artifacts and even artificial organs are made and artificial worlds created. By means of genetic

---

35. Cf. note 13.

manipulation plants, animals and human beings can be made or imitated. Everything, or almost everything, seems imitable, including the human voice, language and intelligence. In all these forms of imitation, what is at issue is mimesis. It can not be reduced to imitation in the sense of the so-called unreal, or simulated.

Plato thinks he can solve things in this way, but this definition would ultimately result in the assertion that *everything* is unreal, or at least everything that really exists and does not belong to the realm of the ideal. But here again a distinction must be made between different forms of mimesis. One of the many questions that obtrude here asks for the exact meanings of the words real and unreal. Even more important is the question if and, above all, to what extent a distinction can be made between these two (real and unreal, proper and improper, natural and unnatural). Can what is real and unreal be decided and delimited definitively and with true accuracy? Doesn't everything that can in a certain respect be called real turn out, on further analysis, to be unreal, and vice versa? What is at stake here, among many other things, is the relation between nature and culture. Jean Baudrillard has made many insightful observations concerning this aspect of the problem of the real and the unreal.[36] But he also seems to declare everything in our world to be unreal, what we have called a sham (*simulacre*), which leaves certain philosophical and, more so, ethical questions in a difficult spot. However, this does not change the fact that he offers a perspective worthy of consideration.

---

36. J. Baudrillard, *De la séduction*, Galilée, Paris 1979 [*Seduction*, translated by B. Singer. MacMillan, London 1990].

Mimesis occurs not only in the domain of making and manufacturing (*poesis*), but also in that of doing, acting and events (*praxis*). Deeds may be done again, actions may be repeated and events may happen again. They can be re-enacted ritually and performed again (imitated) on stage. Deeds may really be done again (imitated) and events may really happen again. *L'histoire se répète*. In addition to this, the following may be remarked: Oedipus has murdered his father and taken his mother for a wife many times already and as many times he has come to see who he is, at least in the tragedy and on stage. Has it ever really happened? And doesn't it happen again each day – and then really? In many cases, are the acts that are really performed and the events that really take place anything other than an unconscious and/or ritual and theatrical repetition and imitation of earlier acts and events (whether or not really having been performed or really having happened)? One might also think of wars that are waged and cleaning-up actions that are then carried out, revolts that break out and conflicts that arise, relations that are entered into and later broken off, and views that are held and abjured and held again and abjured again. In history, there is a great deal of imitation and repetition. Here as well, the meaning of the distinction between real and unreal (or possibly between really having happened and not really having happened) is not always very clear.

Instead of real and unreal, original and unoriginal are often spoken of. Now, the fact is that what is called an original act or event only *becomes* original in and through the doubling, or repetition of this reality, act or event – that is to say, in and through mimesis, which makes the origin into an origin and at the same time implies a withdrawal of the origin. The origin as such is never given; it only appears afterwards, in the doubling, in other words, in the withdrawal. As little as one can imagine a word that would be the absolutely first one ever spoken or written and only then subsequently repeated, so little could one imagine a strictly original reality, act or event. For a word to be capable of meaning something, it has to be fundamentally repeatable and recognizable, and it has to refer to other words to which it is committed in order to mean something. It is therefore never simply original. That is probably how matters stand with all that is called original and real.[37]

---

37. I write 'probably' in deference to the fact that there is a theological tradition in which God is seen as the real and true origin. In this case he does not also belong to the appearing. However, there is also another theological tradition in which God does in fact appear, but then in the stories that are told about Him, or 'in passing', which means there where He is not.

V. Examples, Mirrors and Identity

Man, it is said, is a mimetic being. By this it is meant that man has the ability to imitate nature, that is to say, to represent and to render reality and thus, in a sense, to double it, to consummate the workings of nature and so to bring it to perfection. It also refers to the ability to mimic, follow and imitate one's fellow men. Whether the mimetic is an exclusively human feature is debatable. However, it is certain that through this imitation man has made the world into what it is, and this means a cultivated world – in our times, a world controlled by technology. It is also certain that people imitate each other in many respects, that they follow those who they acknowledge as examples and that they repeat what they consider to be an exemplary way of existence.

People imitate each other frequently. This may happen consciously, in which case a certain distance toward oneself and the other is supposed. One imagines oneself in the position of the other and the other is dissociated from his immediate and vital presence. Among other places, this happens in the theater, but also in the theater that everyday life often can be. However, imitating one another may also happen unconsciously. Often without being aware of it, people imitate the behavior and language of others and adopt their opinions and expectations.[38] Children imitate their parents, some

---

38. H. Plessner, in his studies *Zur Anthropologie der Nachahmung*

students imitate their teachers and most scholars imitate other scholars. Practitioners of science follow the example (paradigm) that is held out to them, and in so doing they are very formal, because then it is possible for one to assert whatever one wants to assert, so long as the form into which the assertion is put remains respected. More or less the same can be said of professionals, technicians and artists. However original and inventive (*inventio*) they may sometimes be, they also will have to join in a tradition, which they do by following exemplary forms, and perhaps partially deviating from them, trying out variations and other combinations within the pre-given form. As well, philosophers imitate other philosophers, even if only by quoting them both implicitly and explicitly, taking up their questions and themes and adopting their rhetorical peculiarities and structures of argumentation. Of course, this, like every form of mimesis, may easily lead to mere appearance. It may lead to estrangement, would-be scholarship, pseudo-science, quasi-professionalism, imitation-art and para-philosophy, but at the same time it is a necessary condition for one to realize oneself as a human being, a scholar, a scientist,

---

(1948), *Zur Anthropologie des Schauspielers* (1948) and *Der imitatorische Akt* (1961), all incorporated in *Gesammelte Schriften VII, Ausdruck und menschliche Natur*, herausgegeben von G. Dux, Frankfurt a.M. 1982, makes a sharp distinction between imitating and joining in. According to Plessner, monkeys and parrots, often counted as examples of aping and imitating, do not really imitate but only join in. Real imitating (*Nachahmen*) is the monopoly of man, and it presupposes reflexivity and eccentricity. Although Plessner's observations are extraordinarily interesting, the distinction he makes is not altogether convincing, because reflexivity and eccentricity may well be presupposed in mimesis, but they are also an effect of it.

a professional, an artist or a philosopher, and for one to achieve or produce something. Of course, the above also holds for heroes and saints, soldiers and managers, merchants and beginners.

In moral life as well, the place of the good and the bad example must not be underestimated. It is correct that a truly ethical attitude is something other than following an example, that is to say: acting as others act, but without examples, an ethical consciousness could not come into being. Even Kant, who remains very mistrustful of any form of imitating and following, nonetheless will not deny this.[39] Thus in Christianity there is the question of an 'imitation of Christ' and it is expected of a Christian that he live, act and judge just like the man from Nazareth. For a Christian, sanctity can be nothing but imitation. This can also lead to sanctimoniousness or hypocrisy but, according to Kant, these are always to be preferred to barbarism.

In René Girard, finally, mimesis is declared the general principle by which every sort of phenomena that is at first glance inexplicable and every matter that is hidden to living memory are brought to light.[40] So-called originality

---

39. Kant's theory of mimesis and the theory of the genius, originality, creativity, freedom, imagination and exemplary being that is linked with it, could be the subject of a separate investigation. His philosophy of art, particularly in §§ 46-50 of the *Critique of Judgment*, and his anthropology and practical philosophy make all sorts of subtle distinctions calling for further analysis – such as, for example, that which distinguishes between *Nachahmung, Nachmachung, Nachfolge, Nachaffung*, etc. [The latter terms appear in the cited passages from the *Critique of Judgment* and center on the sense in which an imitation (*Nachahmung*) can lead its beholder beyond the work to what is imitated and, moreover, according to the specific intention and viewpoint of the artist.]
40. R. Girard, *Things Hidden Since the Foundation of the World*, trans.

is exposed as a romantic lie[41] and the perpetrators all go along the same old way.[42] According to Girard, desire has a mimetic structure. It has its origin neither in the desiring subject nor in the desired object, but comes into being through others (the rivals) desiring the desired object. Only thus does an object become desirable.

It is very tempting to interpret the form of mimesis invoked here – that is, mimicking, following or imitating others – according to the traditional scheme of an original example and an unoriginal imitation, or in light of the opposition between real and unreal. It is correct to say that mimesis is characterized by a fundamental ambivalence. It is possible that someone who imitates someone else according to a prescribed protocol, neither daring nor being able to say or do anything not already said or done by others, becomes estranged from himself, loses himself and founders in a world of appearance – or, even worse, never becomes himself and never rises above the world of this appearance. However, in mimesis other possibilities lie hidden which can not be reduced to the opposition between real and unreal, or original and not original.

With regard to the example that someone follows, it has to be said that it is never simply original. It only becomes an example in and through the imitating, and it is itself always already an effect or result of imitation. Further, it may happen that in and through imitation, the

S. Bann and M. Metteer. Athlone Press, London 1987.
41. R. Girard, *Mensonge romantique et vérité romanesque*. Grasset, Paris 1961.
42. R. Girard, *La route antique des hommes pervers*. Grasset, Paris 1985.

one who is imitated will appear in a new or different way. In the theater, personages are represented which come to life in that representation, and in conscious imitation someone's features that had gone unnoticed before will now stand out. A similar thing also happens in imitation that is unconscious or not expressly willed. The one who imitates functions, as it were, as a mirror in which the one who is imitated is reflected and can thus appear to himself and others. Sometimes to his surprise and sometimes to his annoyance, he can recognize himself in his mirror-image, and others can see him as he appears to be.

Something happens to the one who mimics, follows or imitates which is not of the order of real and unreal, but is rather something like the obtaining of a certain identity. As we remarked earlier, in conscious imitation a distance is supposed toward oneself and the other. One tries to imagine oneself in the position of the other and to identify with him. This means that a doubling appears which is supposed and effected in the imitation. The imitator is (becomes) himself because he *imitates* the other, and is (becomes) someone else because he imitates *the other*.

A doubling also appears in the imitating or following which is not expressly willed, where the distance is usually smaller. Here the one who is followed functions as a mirror in which the follower sees himself reflected. He identifies with the example (the image) held out to him.[43] In and through this identification one obtains a

---

43. [Here there is a play on the resonances between the Dutch *beeld* (image) and *voorbeeld* (example) which can not be translated directly into English. IJsseling highlights the sense in which the

proper identity or ownness on the ground of which one can be distinguished from others. In so far as one identifies with an example or mirror-image, this identity has an imaginary character. And in so far as it is accompanied by a doubling and is and remains committed to the other, it is broken and derived. This other, in its/his turn is just as much the effect of mimesis, and can only occur as the other on the ground of mimesis.

Identity therefore neither exists in the full possession of oneself nor in pure presence to oneself, but is appropriated and assigned in mimesis, and this appropriation and assignment are attended by a dispossession and an absence. In other words, in mimesis man discovers and reveals himself and reality. Through it, man can present himself to himself and to others as he is, and reality can appear as it appears. At the same time, something withdraws and something is taken from man and reality, something that he has in fact never possessed – namely, full coincidence with himself. The ground-structure of mimesis, as we have described it in relation to drama and literature, art and rendering, re-producing and reenacting, comes together here.

The process of identification is extremely complicated, and to realize some of its complexity it would be desirable to read what Freud has written on identification and what, according to him, is connected to it, such as aggression and regression, interiorization and super-ego, rivalry and idealization, repetition and imagination, mourning and melancholy, name-giving and having a

---

image with which one identifies is one that is already there, held out in advance, a 'pre-image' (*voor-beeld*).]

place in a story. It is not possible here to enter into Freud's subtle analyses. However, in connection with Freud and the problem of mimesis it is important to see that it is not entirely correct to speak of identifying *oneself* with someone, because this 'oneself' from which the identification would begin is an effect of a (primary) identification and does not precede it. In a sense, then, one *is* identified.[44] In this, an important part is played by the mirror.

Henceforth from the moment that, with the Greeks, the problem of mimesis was set, it has been seen in connection with the mirror. Just like mimesis, the mirror – and there are many kinds of mirrors – occupies an important place in culture. From of old, the ambivalence of mimesis has been recognized and, because of this, people have always taken an ambivalent attitude toward it. The same can be said of the mirror. The mirror, 'in which everything happens and nothing is remembered', according to a beautiful phrase of Borges,[45] is seen as an object in which reality and each change in reality is represented in the most perfect way, but at the same time, the mirror-image is understood as the most unreal and deceptive. In the mirror, people and things appear where they are not.

---

44. Freud makes all kinds of distinctions in the process of identification which are important for the problem of mimesis. His *Massenpsychologie und Ich-Analyse* (1921) is of particular importance in this scope. In S. Freud, *Gesammelte Werke*, Imago, London 1940-1952, Band XIII 71-161 [*The Standard Edition of the Complete Psychological Works of Sigmund Freud*, translated by J. Strachey, The Hogarth Press, London 1953-1974, vol. XVII, pp. 69-143].
45. J.L. Borges, El Hacedor, in *Obras Completas*, Emecé, Buenos Aires 1974 [reference is to a short story called 'The Mirrors.']

The mirror is seen as a symbol of vanity, moral decay, self-love and self-destruction – remember the story of Narcissus – but also of self-knowledge, self-restraint and self-control.[46] It is a device which enables man to see whether he can appear in public. The mirror is seen as the pre-eminent domain of appearance, and the mirror-image as the most evanescent and transitory. But there is also a widespread metaphoric in which the 'soul', the 'subject' and the 'spirit' are called a mirror of reality, which is to say: a place where reality becomes visible and where it can appear. Thus, for Leibniz monads are mirrors which more or less sharply reflect the universe, and in Hegel's *speculative* idealism the Absolute is understood as reality's being perfectly reflected in itself. In summary, the mirror, and it is *the* example of mimesis, is seen as the place of appearance (*doxa*) but also as the place of appearing, and perhaps appearing is another word for being.[47]

There are many kinds of mirrors. There are man-made mirrors: objects of polished metal or of glass to the back of which a certain preparation (foil) is applied, that, by reflection, mirror images of other objects that are in front of it in one manner or another. The function of these mirrors is to make man visible to himself and to let reality appear through a doubling.[48] These mirrors

---

46. C. Verhoeven, 'Narcissus, een jager in de spiegel', [= 'Narcissus, a Hunter in the Mirror'] in: *Voorbij het begin. De Griekse filsofie in haar spiegel. 2. Termen en thema's.* Ambo, Baarn 1985, pp. 11-44.
47. 'Der *Schein* selbst is dem *Wesen* wesentlich, die Wahrheit wäre nicht, wenn sie nicht schiene und erschiene.' In Hegel, *Ästhetik*, p. 21 [*Aesthetics*, vol. I, pp. 7-8.]
48. 'A certain kind of man-made mirror is called psyche, or cheval-glass. It is a large mirror, supported on a frame and able to swivel

are imitated after the examples of mirrors that are found in nature, and they are a perfection of them. The outstanding example of a natural mirror is a sheet of water, a pond or a lake, but in fact every shining object that mirrors images by reflection is a mirror.[49] The man-made and the natural mirror – this distinction is not always very clear – play a large part in society. They function in everyday life and social interaction, they are used in all kinds of research and technical skills, and

---

on a horizontal axis, in which one can see oneself from head to foot. What is called the principle of life (psyche, soul) appears to have something to do with mirrors. This is expressed in a widespread metaphoric in which a part is played by the belonging together of soul and mirror, of interior and exterior, and the continuous change of their position. Also because of this metaphoric – and this latter is itself another word for transposition – Derrida has chosen the word "psyche" as the title of one of his books: *Psychè. Inventions de l'autre.* Galilée, Paris 1987.

49. Only an extremely small portion of mirror-images that are reflected is perceived. Consequently, it seems as if they are not reflected, but this can not be stated. However mysterious it may sound, as long as there is any light at all, the trees around a pond in the woods are reflected in an endless number of perspectives, even if there is no passer-by to see them. Where are these mirror-images? Neither in the trees nor in the pond. But then where? Not in the eyes of the passer-by, for he isn't there, and even if he were he would only see one image. At the slightest movement of his glance that first image is no longer there for him and another has taken its place. Where has that first image gone, and from where has the second one come? Perhaps all of this supplies an indication for what we may call the reality of anything whatsoever. Cf. *Le Séminaire de Jacques Lacan. Livre II. Le moi dans la théorie de Freud et dans la technique de la psychanalyse*, ed. J.-A. Miller. Seuil, Paris 1978, pp. 61-62 [*The Seminar of Jacques Lacan. Book II. The Ego in the Theory of Freud and in the Technique of Psychoanalysis*, ed. J.-A. Miller, trans. S. Tomaselli, with notes by J. Forrester. Cambridge University Press, Cambridge, UK 1988, pp 46-47].

they have their place in art and architecture.[50] When we look around, in fact we discover mirrors everywhere. In a certain respect, it can even be said that *every* object is a mirror, because it reflects light, but in many cases the light spreads in many different directions so that no images are reflected, while shiny objects reflect light rays more or less in a single direction, bringing into being more or less sharp images of the objects that reflect or give out light themselves. Without entering into the intricate, technical details,[51] it may be said that in and through the mirror reality appears in one way or another, and in fact as an image, a rendering.

When one sees oneself in a mirror, an image is held up to oneself. This image also determines the image one has of oneself when not in front of the mirror and allows for the experience of oneself as a (broken) unity and a (decentered) center of all one's doings. One recognizes the image as one's own and identifies with it. This recognition and identification are essential for obtaining a personal identity. In this connection, Jacques Lacan speaks of the *stade du miroir* [mirror-stage].[52] What is at issue here in the first instance is a phase in the consti-

---

50. In the visual arts mirrors are often represented along with all of their connected effects. In garden architecture ponds are often used because they reflect trees and buildings, and in modern high-rises windows reflect the surroundings which give a modern city its specific character.
51. An account of numerous technical aspects of the mirror can be found in U. Eco, *Über Spiegel und andere Phänomene*. Hanser Verlag, München/Wien 1988, especially pp. 26-61.
52. J. Lacan, 'Le stade-miroir comme formateur de la fonction du je', in *Ecrits*, Seuil, Paris 1966, pp. 93-100 ['The Mirror-Stage as Formative for the Function of the I', in his *Ecrits. A Selection*, trans. A. Sheridan. Tavistock, London 1977, pp. 1-7].

tution of human being that is supposed to take place between the sixth and eighteenth month, in which the child, as yet neither able to coordinate its movements nor experiencing its body as a unity, anticipates this unity in an imaginary way by identifying with the image which the other (his equal) holds out to him. This identification is actualized in the concrete and in a way pleasurable to the child who sees and recognizes himself in the mirror. According to Lacan, this phase is the matrix and basic pattern of what will be the 'I'.[53] In Lacan, this is not only a phase that one should ever go through and then leave behind for good, but it is also an essential structure of being human. Each time man recognizes himself in one way or another in – and identifies with – an image of himself that is held out to him, in principle the same process repeats itself, namely obtaining an identity which is imaginary in nature because it is an identification with an image.[54]

---

53. J. Laplanche and J.-B. Pontalis, *Vocabulaire de la psychanalyse*, PUF, Paris 1967, pp. 452-453 [*The Language of Psychoanalysis*, translated by D. Nicholson-Smith. Hogarth, London 1973, p. 252-252].

54. Lacan makes a distinction between the real, the imaginary and the symbolic. According to him, the real is not accessible; it is the impossible. The imaginary is that which is called reality in everyday language. The symbolic is first of all the order of speech. At times Lacan tends to regard the imaginary as inferior. This may have its ground in an 'existential' tendency to retain a certain ideal of authenticity. If one takes mimesis seriously, as we try to do here, there can be no such thing as inferiority. But, indeed, the imaginary, like the mimetic, is polyvalent. There are forms of the imaginary which are in fact based on fancy, such as certain fears, but this can not be said of the imaginary or the mimetic *as such*. Cf. Ph. van Haute, *Psychoanalyse en Filosofie*, Peeters, Leuven 1989.

It is not only in man-made (imitated) and natural mirrors that an image is reflected to man of who and what he is. There are a number of other possibilities to hold out an image of what one is, ought or would wish to be. Many of these are called mirrors as well. Thus, one may speak of an 'emperor's mirror',[55] that is to say a manual in which the image of a sovereign is sketched and to which a good sovereign should answer. Such mirrors have existed for almost every manner of human existence and every professional branch, often without it being realized, in the form of implicit or explicit expectations and prevailing role-patterns. *Il cortegiano* (the courtier), a book from the beginning of the sixteenth century by the Italian author B. Castiglione, has very clearly functioned as a mirror.[56] In all sorts of versions, adapted versions and translations it has played an important part in European culture. An image is sketched of what it is to appear well-mannered, eloquent and right-minded. It is a mirror that enables man to appear in public and to behave 'courteously.' Many manuals of rhetoric and etiquette have functioned in more or less the same way.

Shakespeare has said of the theater that 'the purpose of playing, whose end, both at the first and now, was and is, to hold as 'twere, the mirror up to nature; to show virtue her own feature, scorn her own image, and the very age and body of the time his form and pressure.'[57] In the theater (and in film) reality is reflected and a mirror is

---

55. [This translates literally '*Vorsten-spiegel*', for which there is no equivalent expression in English idiom. The context, however, makes clear its meaning.]
56. P. Burke, *op. cit.*
57. W. Shakespeare, *Hamlet* III, 2.

held out to people. This can also be said of most of the mimetic arts, the visual arts and literature, and of the stories that go around about man and his world. They are a reflection or rendering of reality, which is thus revealed in a certain way. They are decisive for the way in which man sees or experiences this reality or, what amounts to the same thing, for the way reality appears to him. To a certain extent this also holds for the great philosophical systems. They function as mirrors in which man sees reality reflected and his place within it.

However, mirrors are not only revealing, but also concealing. In this very revealing there is also and at the same time much concealing. The cinema, it is said, is a dream factory. With regard to the visual arts we speak of an aesthetic illusion and with regard to stories an epic illusion. And, according to Kant, philosophy is threatened and accompanied by a transcendental appearance.

Different things may be meant by aesthetic illusion. Thus, for example, with the help of technical means, a painter can bring about certain effects, such as the suggestion of space and depth, unity and coherence, and the presence of things and people which are not there and are not represented. By aesthetic illusion it may also be meant that the artist offers a more beautiful, nobler and more reassuring image of reality than is in fact the case. Art can protect us against the harshness of existence and, as Freud said, it can work as a *narcotic*.[58] Thus Nietzsche writes: 'Art is there for us so that we do not perish from the truth.'[59]

---

58. S. Freud, 'Das Unbehagen in der Kultuur' in *Gesammelte Werke* XIV, p. 439 ['Civilization and Its Discontents', in *The Standard Edition*, vol. XXI, p. 81].

59. F. Nietzsche, *Wille zur Macht*, §822, in Werke III 852; Nietzsche's

Epic illusion points at the phenomena whereby a story, which has a beginning and an end and displays a certain unity and coherence, makes into a whole events which are perfectly fortuitous, incoherent, disordered, irrational and even irreconcilable. The world becomes tellable by bestowing on it a beginning and end, unity and coherence. The 'great narratives' of which Jean-François Lyotard speaks are even capable of putting into words the origin and completion, the meaning and the ultimate end of total reality. Because of this epic illusion many philosophers, among them Plato, are particularly suspicious of any kind of story in philosophy.[60] And on the grounds of what unreasonableness we have experienced in the twentieth century, Lyotard says that the 'great narratives', however impressive they may be, in fact no longer function.[61]

Besides the danger of falling into the storytelling which, according to many philosophers, threatens us, Kant sees an even more fundamental and, for him, ineradicable

---

interpretations of mimesis requires a separate fundamental analysis. These interpretations move beyond the opposition between real and imitation or truth and appearance. In many texts, art is accorded a higher place than is truth: the *Birth of Tragedy* speaks of an art that 'is not merely imitatation of reality, but a metaphysical *supplement* standing alongside this reality in order to overcome it' (*Werke I*, p. 130). On this, see also S. IJsseling, 'Nietzsche en de rhetorica', in *Tijdschrift voor Filosofie* 35(1973), pp. 766-799.

60. Plato, *Republic* X, 378-379. It is interesting to note that Lyotard's distinction between great and small narratives is made already here.

61. J.-F. Lyotard, *La condition postmoderne. Rapport sur le savoir*. Minuit, Paris 1979 [*The Postmodern Condition. A Report on Knowledge*, trans. G. Bennington and B. Massumi. University of Minnesota Press, Minneapolis, MN 1984].

danger – that of transcendental appearance. By this, he refers to a innate tendency among philosophers to give a perfectly coherent and logically accountable exposition, and to hold it true without either premises or results being in any way verifiable by experience. The mirror which philosophy then holds out to people is a magnificent palace of concepts, but one in which, in the end, man cannot live.[62]

The word 'illusion' may not always be equally appropriate to indicate the phenomena just now described. It could suggest that beneath or behind the illusion a true reality could appear without any form of mimesis. Doubtless, some illusions may be unmasked, but not by discovering an original, proper and real reality behind the mimesis. The concealing but also revealing character of every mirror – including that mirror which is the theater, art, the story and philosophy – exists in the first place such that reality always appears where it in fact is not, namely in the mirror, on the stage, in the work of art, in the story or in the philosophical system. The appearance of reality there where it is not probably belongs to the very structure of the appearance of all that is called reality. This is what a radical reflection on mimesis teaches us.

---

62. I. Kant, *Critique of Pure Reason*, B. 352-353.

VI. Mimesis and Intertextuality

In the tradition, two forms of mimesis are usually distinguished and opposed: the so-called imitation of nature (*mimesis tes phuseoos, imitatio naturae*) and the imitation of other, older and exemplary authors or possibly artists, professionals and so on (*mimesis toon archaioon, imitatio veterum*). This distinction and this opposition are found in nearly all dictionaries, manuals and studies which treat of mimesis. However, on closer analysis this opposition appears to be somewhat problematic – namely, that the problem of mimesis is not posed radically and, furthermore, that a (metaphysical) view of reality is held which is itself affected in its foundations by a thinking through of the mimetic.

Traditionally, the mimesis of nature has meant the entire domain of rendering, representing, depicting, imitating and perfecting of what is called reality. We have already seen that this concerns extremely intricate relations and distinctions which are almost impossible to unravel. Mimesis of the ancients has meant the domain of following, mimicking and imitating other authors, artists, professionals, etc. Dionysius of Halicarnassus (born around 60 BC) has written a work about this second form of mimesis which has come down to us in fragments and is entitled *Peri mimeseoos* (*de imitatione*). There, mimesis means first of all that to be a good writer and speaker, one must follow and imitate the great writers and orators considered exemplary. This imitation bears on style, composition and choice of words, but also on the subjects and themes to be treated, and is characterized by emulation (*zelos*), a striving to exceed the example. According to Dionysius, this imitation can be natural, which would mean that it is based on lasting intercourse with (the texts of) exemplary writers, but it can also be based on technical instruction. It is not possible to elaborate further here on the other aspects of imitation as put forth by this author, nor on the problems of interpretation posed by these fragments. But what can indeed be said is that the plea for imitation of exemplary writers returns frequently throughout the rhetorical and literary tradition from the ancients on up to the beginning of modernity. One finds it already in the Sophists and Isocrates; it is an important theme in Quintilian[63] and it belongs to the essence of the Renaissance. Sometimes, for example in Horace,[64] the herd of servile imitators (*imitatorum servum pecus*) is mocked and the emphasis is on the fact that the imitation should not be a repetition, but should be accompanied by the attempt to say the same in another way (*variatio*), striving to exceed the example (*aemulatio*). But the idea of imitation is thought highly of, which does not change until the age of Romanticism. It is only then that originality is glorified – an originality that is exposed as a 'romantic lie' by Rene Girard.

The domain of the imitation of the other covers much more than that of the art of writing and speaking, but it bears on all the arts, on technical skills, practical and

---

63. Quintilian, *Institutionis oratiorae* liber XII, book X, 2.
64. Horace, *Epistulae*, 1, 9.

theoretical possibilities and also on the art of life. All of this must be learned and, according to the rhetorical tradition, all learning is first and foremost imitating.[65] In order not to overcomplicate things, in what follows we will limit ourselves in the first instance to the art of writing and reading. However, what is said here does hold, *mutatis mutandis*, for the arts in general. A number of things that have risen before will return here, albeit in another frame.

The imitation of exemplary writers involves many things. The desire to write and eventually to publish is already mimetic. It has its origin neither in the inner self of the author nor in the attractiveness of publication itself, but comes about because others seem to find writing and publishing attractive. Because the possibilities for publishing are scarce, one is sometimes prepared to make great sacrifices for the chance to belong to the small group of people who have published a book or at least an article.[66] As soon as one is won over by the idea of writing something, one begins to carry out all sorts of ritual actions which are of a mimetic nature. To these belong, among other things, being seated in a particular way,

---

65. The model for all learning, according to the rhetorical tradition (and the Sophists), is learning the mother tongue. Learning is a process of assimilation in which being together with the teacher (*sunousia*) and imitating him are of great importance. Plato sets a different model against this, the insight of mathematics. This insight is to be found in oneself. Cf. Th. Buchheim, *Die Sophistik als Avantgarde normalen Lebens*, Hamburg, F. Meiner Verlag, pp. 123-127.

66. This is one of the themes of Umberto Eco's *Foucault's Pendulum*, trans. by W. Leaven, Secker and Warburg, London 1989.

holding one's pen or possibly operating a typewriter or word processor, and many other activities that a writer imitates from other writers. The preparation of a manuscript follows an intricate system of prescriptions that functions as an example or a mirror. These prescriptions bear on the use of a particular kind of script, spelling and punctuation marks, to which also belong the capitals at the beginning of each sentence, quotation marks and the grouping of chapters and paragraphs. In some cases, the text is provided with a table of contents, a preface or postface, footnotes, a bibliography and an index, sometimes a motto and a dedication and, since the invention of printing, a title.

Furthermore, there are prescriptions pertaining to size and construction, grammar and style, the manner of describing and reasoning, the use of formulas and examples, etc. It is also of great importance to know beforehand the genre to which what one writes should belong, since prescriptions differ from genre to genre. It is therefore not a matter of indifference whether one writes a story or a treatise, an informative text or a philosophical text. Nor is it unimportant whether something is written for a scroll or a bound book, for a book that is meant to be read aloud or quietly, for a scientific magazine or newspaper. Of course, it is also possible to deviate from these prescriptions – some authors, like Nietzsche, are masters at it – with this deviation belonging to the *variatio*. It is important to see that these and other such prescriptions have a long history, that they make a text as text possible and that they determine the production of meaning.

When one proceeds to publication, there is once again a prescribed scenario to be followed. One enters the public sphere, which is characterized by rituals and juridical obligations, among which also belong copyright and the plagiarism associated with it. Generally, the author parts with his manuscript and has little to say about material design. To the latter belong, besides the choice of typeface, text space, binding, etc., determination of the number of copies printed, their price and the organization of distribution.[67] In all of this, examples are once again followed, and intricate mimetic relations are involved.

In the development and understanding of a text – in other words, in writing and manufacturing and reading – still more is at stake. Just as one can not think of or picture a single object or event without other objects or events to which reference is made and to which an object or event is committed in order to be or occur, so too one can not imagine or think of a word, phrase or text that does not somehow refer to other words, phrases or texts, and is not somehow committed to them in order to be spoken or written, heard or read. The meaning of a word or text is outlined in and through coherence and distinction with regard to other words and texts.

This reference and commitment is also called intertextuality. This is perhaps a variant and radicalization of the *imitatio veterum*. Here it is a matter of the place of a text in the whole of texts or of the relation of a particular text to a network of texts. This place and relation are

---

67. It is important not to underestimate all of these exterior and material aspects of a text. They play an essential role in the realization of meanings. A philosophy of language which disregards these aspects does not speak of language but of ideas. Language, in short, is exteriority and materiality.

50

mimetic in nature. In order for a text to be written and read, it is necessary that it imitate a great deal. Without this imitation, which is characterized by repeating and assuming the same but in a slightly different way, a text could be neither written nor read. There is no zero-point in writing, for writing always presupposes that there has already been something related which is already written; there is no zero-point in reading because reading is always already having read.

The mimetic structures above can be found in every text. In philosophical texts they are even highlighted. With some irony, one might even say that the only texts which philosophers accept as truly philosophical are those in which other philosophers are cited, supported or challenged, commented on or interpreted, clarified or improved, summarized or amplified, supplemented or shortened. All of these are mimetic activities elaborately taken up in classical rhetoric. The greatness of the philosophical tradition consists in repeating what is always the same (that is, the fundamental questions of philosophy), but each time in a slightly different way. One of the weak points of a metaphysics which asks immediately for the truth and of a hermeneutics which asks exclusively for the meaning is that they have little or no eye for the text as text or for its material and differential aspects, while it is precisely these that make the production of meaning possible.

Many philosophers have a rather ideological (in the sense of *les Idéologues*) and idealist conception of language and text that is closely interwoven with a 'refusal' to pose the questions of mimesis and a lack of reflection on the acts of reading and writing.[68] For many among them, the

---

68. It is most surprising that in philosophy very little attention is paid

word is a sign at the disposal of man which stands for a thought which is given outside the order of signs and present at his interior, or for a reality which is present in the exterior world. However, reflection on mimesis indicates, as we have seen, that language is not simply at the disposal of man, that rendering and the rendered are not fully outside of each other and that neither thought nor reality is given without any form of rendering.

One aspect of the reference and commitment mentioned above is what is called context.[69] Each text has a context which is linguistic as well as real, and which, according to an old hermeneutic rule, is jointly determinate for the meaning. On the one hand, a context is always specific, particular and in a certain sense demonstrable, but on the other hand it is never exhaustively determinable or fully delimitable. Thus, the context can in essence be extended to all sides without end. The limits at which one allows a context to begin and end are

---

to the acts of reading and writing, especially when one compares this to the attention paid to perception. It is all the more surprising because by far the majority of the philosopher's activities consists in reading and writing. Perhaps it is too threatening. Once one has an eye for this problem, one notices that almost all great philosophers allude to these acts. Furthermore, there is at work in philosophy a widespread metaphoric in which letters, inscriptions, the (white) paper, the book (of the world), the text, the margin, reading, etc., constantly return. Cf. S. IJsseling, 'Fenomenologie, hermeneutiek en retoriek', in: Th. de Boer, et. al., *Fenomenologie en kritiek*, Assen 1981, pp. 48-59.

69. On this, cf. J. Derrida, 'Signature événement contexte', in *Marges de la philosophie*, Minuit, Paris 1972, pp. 365-393 ['Signature Event Context', in *Margins of Philosophy*, trans., with additional notes, by A. Bass. University of Chicago Press 1982, pp. 309-330].

always drawn arbitrarily and can always be altered. In that delimitation something fundamentally undecidable is nonetheless decided. However, each text can also be taken out of its actual context and put in another, so that the same text comes to function in a another way and different meanings are produced. This possibility of being taken out of context is essential for all speaking and writing and all intelligibility and legibility.

As Plato already noted, the act of taking out of context is an instance of repetition and has a mimetic structure. It can take place by explicit or implicit citation, recitation, reproduction, etc., but reading and understanding are also repetition, a resumption of what has been written or said earlier by oneself or others. It is a resumption at another moment and in a different place than the moment and place in which something was written or said. It may also be noted here that all citing and all repeating – and one can neither read and write nor speak and understand without quoting and repeating in one way or another – is *always* a taking away, a cutting off from an 'original' context and a letting function in another context, through which are produced meanings other than the 'originals'. Quoting, and more generally repeating, is thus about a same identical word or text, but with 'same' and 'identical' being relative concepts here, just as is 'original.' And things become even more complicated when several, possibly even many thousands of copies of one and the same text exist. Then, each separate copy is a copy of the same text, but also occupies a place of its own in the spatio-temporal world and has its own context through which it produces meanings in its own way specific to that context.

Because of the fact that, on the one hand, each text has

a context which jointly determines the meaning, and that, on the other hand, the context can never be fully delimited and therefore can produce other meanings, it is the case that a meaning is never – nor ever can be – fully fixed, and that the production of meaning always to some extent escapes from a writer or speaker. Derrida speaks here of *dissemination*, which is to be distinguished from polysemy.[70] Polysemy refers to a multitude of meanings that are essentially governable and controllable. The many and different meanings can be determined and registered. Dissemination is about the phenomenon that the production of meaning is never fully controllable. In no way is this then to say that everything can mean everything so that in fact nothing means anything anymore. To the contrary, in writing and speaking one must try to control and master the production of meaning to the utmost and in every detail. Especially when one does so will it appear to be impracticable. Writing is therefore an extremely laborious occupation, particularly so in the case of a philosophical text. One has to know, see, realize and even foresee a great deal. One has to survey in all its presuppositions and consequences the entire domain on which one writes. All words must, as we say, be weighed on a golden scale. But at the same time much must be forgotten, not seen, not understood, and left to what is uncontrollable and cannot be weighed. This also counts for reading. The reader must try to understand everything that is said, word for word, but understanding as well as understandability are essentially limited. Writing and reading are forms of appropriation,

---

70. *ibid.*, p. 392.

but this is always accompanied by expropriation. Something is taken from man and reality which they have never possessed, namely complete coincidence with oneself. Perhaps the words appropriation and expropriation summarize what takes place in every form of mimesis.

In the tradition, as we have already said, imitation of the other is usually opposed to imitation of or rendering of nature or of reality. From what we have seen above, it becomes apparent that this opposition is somewhat problematic. Of course, when wishing to describe a harbor – the example comes from the rhetorical tradition – consulting other authors is not the same thing as going to take a look for oneself. And yet the difference is less clear than one may think. In the first place, even if one does go to look for oneself, it is impossible to give a description of what one has seen without appealing to already existing descriptions, if only because one must use words which are already the words of others. Indeed, most repeated words are in fact nobody's words, words without an author. However, not only the words, but also the very act of describing and its formal structure are taken up anew, whereby the *variatio* may play an important role. Moreover, the author who imitates exemplary authors in the sense described above does positively imitate reality, namely the reality which is the imitated author himself. Possibly, he resumes, repeats and perfects the very real and in many respects material process of the construction of a work. One might further ask oneself whether there would be anything to see if one went to look for oneself without knowing where and how to look. Knowing where and how to look for something is made possible by preliminary forms of rendering which reflect reality and show it as it is. In other words: reality could not appear as it appears without the word of the poet that is itself mimetic and without the work of those who have made the world into what it is. In all this, one must not forget that the 'harbor' itself is already a human construction, a reproduction of other natural or artificial harbors.

What is ultimately at stake here is the appearance of reality. It concerns the problem of *doxa*, a word which is preferably not translated as (subjective) opinion, but rather has something to do with occurring, showing oneself, emerging, appearing, distinguishing oneself and being distinguishable, or perhaps with shining or gleaming. Thus, in the New Testament and in Hellenistic theology one speaks of the *doxa theou*, which is translated as the glory or magnificence of God, and at times there is talk of the *doxa* of man, which means something like his fame, esteem, renown.[71] This *doxa* is closely connected with the *logos*, which in this case means the hymn [doxology] sung in praise of God and the stories which are told about man. This *logos* is a kind of mirror in which God and man appear.

We have repeatedly emphasized that the mirror is the outstanding example of mimesis. It is the place where reality appears where it is not, and where 'everything happens and nothing is remembered' (Borges). When we spoke just now of the *logos* which functions as a mirror, this is indeed a mirror where God, man and any other being appear where they are not. However, in this mirror

---

71. Cf. S. IJsseling, 'Macht, taal en begeerte', in *Tijdschrift voor Filosofie* 41(1979), pp. 381-382.

there is remembrance. Remembrance which, according to Paul Valéry, is the substance of all thought,[72] and in which perhaps nothing happens but everything is repeated and saved, is again mimetic.[73] Fantasy or productive imagination, which is a condition of the possibility of most forms of mimesis and plays a large part in the arts, is also mimetic. This is not the place to enter into the question of whether remembrance and imagination are always attended by images – in fact, on further analysis this turns out not to be the case –, but it may be stated that in remembrance and imagination there is always a doubling, a repeating and a recognizing.

Furthermore, understanding, perception and experience, which are not possible without remembrance and imagination, have a mimetic dimension. A close analysis of the act of seeing, which has an essentially temporal structure, shows that in order to see something as something, a continuation and repetition of that act must take place. Seeing is already having seen, as Aristotle remarks.[74] The same can be said of every form of learning, perceiving and experiencing. Speaking about a first and original perception or experience only makes sense when

---

72. P. Valéry, 'Poetry and Abstract Thought', in his *The Art of Poetry*, Routledge and Kegan Paul, London 1958. [The essay cited here is a Zaharoof lecture delivered by Valéry at Oxford University in 1939. The original French version can be found in P. Valéry, *Oeuvres* I, ed. and ann. J. Hytier]

73. '...Mnémosyne et Mimesis sont difficiles à discerner.' J.-L. Nancy, 'Le ventriloque', in *Mimesis des articulations*, Aubier-Flammarion, Paris 1975, p. 337.

74. Aristotle, *Metaphysics* VI 1048b. Cited by M. Heidegger, 'Vom Wesen und Begriff der Physis', in *Wegmarken*, Gesamtausgabe Band 9, p. 355 [Heidegger's Gesamtausgabe cited hereafter as GA].

others have succeeded it and which are a repetition and resumption of the first, but without ever fully coinciding with it. It is on the grounds of this repetition and this not fully coinciding – and this means on the grounds of identity and difference – that learning, perceiving and experiencing are possible. This is also the reason why there can be no question of an absolute presence. Each presence is essentially imbued with an absence. Every appropriation is attended by an expropriation.

One may be inclined to object that when mimesis is conceived in such a broad sense it becomes all-embracing and meaningless. To a certain extent it is indeed correct that mimesis can be shown everywhere. The mimetic belongs to a manner in which appear the being which we ourselves are and the being which we are not. Therefore, the domain of mimesis admits no clear definition or delimitation, so that every translation of this word is problematic. But this does not at all deny that in mimesis all sorts of distinctions can and should be made. Just as there is an indeterminable multitude of ways of appearing, so there is also a multiplicity of forms of mimesis branching out in every direction. The foregoing is an attempt to create some order in this multiplicity. In philosophy there is always a way up and a way down, of which Heraclitus already said that they are one and the same. Small stretches of this way may have been covered in the preceding pages, but many problems remain unsolved. One such problem is the fundamental ambivalence of all that is mimetic. Instead of ambivalence, one might rather speak of polyvalence or of a cluster of matters which are related to and distinct from one another, the sum of which can not be unravelled. With that, however, the problem remains unsolved.

VII. Heidegger and Mimesis

Many philosophers of the twentieth century, including Benjamin, Adorno, Plessner and Ricoeur, have paid considerable attention to mimesis. For understandable reasons, the problem of mimesis occupies a privileged position in the work of authors who are sometimes singled out as the philosophers of difference and who allow themselves to be inspired by Heidegger – authors such as Derrida and Lacoue-Labarthe. In the work of Heidegger, however, there is seldom mention of mimesis. True, in twenty pages from the lectures on Nietzsche explicit mention is made of the problem of mimesis, but there Heidegger gives only a clear, yet limited and rather traditional rendering of Plato's ideas.[75] In Plato's conception of mimesis Heidegger sees a shadow of his doctrine of truth as correspondence (*homoiosis*). And in his *Introduction to Metaphysics*, he juxtaposes the latter with mimesis.[76]

Heidegger's reserve with respect to mimesis is radical and most surprising. Almost all fundamental ideas of Greek philosophy are either submitted to a critical analysis by Heidegger or made fruitful again in a *Wiederholung*

---

75. M. Heidegger, *Nietzsche I*, Neske, Pfüllingen 1961, pp. 198-217 [*Nietzsche*, vol. I, translated by D.F. Krell. Harper and Row, New York 1979, pp. 171-187.].
76. M. Heidegger, *Einführung in die Metaphysik*, Niemeyer, Tübingen 1953, p. 141 [*An Introduction to Metaphysics*, translated by R. Mannheim, Yale University Press, New Haven 1959, p. 185].

[retrieval] which lets them say what they would have said originally. About mimesis, however, he remains silent. Nowhere does he invoke it to clarify what happens in poetry, art, technology and politics, and nowhere in his many elaborate expositions on *doxa* is there any reference to it. This reservedness even goes so far that in his *Vom Wesen und Begriff der Physis*, citing a long passage from Aristotle's *Physics*, Heidegger breaks off the citation exactly where Aristotle comes to speak about mimesis.[77] Heidegger's 'refusal' to pose the question of mimesis parallels his negative attitude toward the Sophists (and Roman philosophy in its entirety). According to Heidegger, the Sophists have no relation whatsoever to *alètheia*.[78] Their philosophy is one of common sense and is characterized by the absence of serious questions.[79] Sophistry is a deterioration of philosophy,[80] and for the Sophists everything is *Verdeckung* [covering-up], *Verstellung* [disguise], *Verdrehung* [distortion], *Verfallenheit* [fallenness] and *Gerede* [idle talk].[81] Heidegger's stand-

---

77. M. Heidegger, 'Vom Wesen und Begriff der Physis', in *Wegmarken*. GA Band 9, pp. 239-240.

78. M. Heidegger, *Logik. Die Frage nach Wahrheit*, GA Band 21. Klostermann, Frankfurt a.M. 1976, p. 19.

79. M. Heidegger, 'Vom Wesen der Wahrheit', in *Wegmarken*, GA Band 9, Klostermann, Frankfurt a.M. 1976, p. 199 ['On The Essence of Truth', translated by J. Sallis, in *Martin Heidegger. The Basic Writings*, ed. D.F. Krell. Harper and Row, New York 1977, p. 138].

80. M. Heidegger, *Nietzsche II*, Neske, Pfüllingen 1961, pp. 135-171 [*Nietzsche*, vol. IV, translated by D.F. Krell. Harper and Row, New York, 1984, pp. 91-95] This text on the Sophists is later taken up almost literally, though with several important changes, in Heidegger's *Holzwege*, Klostermann, Frankfurt a.M., pp. 94-98.

81. Heidegger distinguishes these terms in his *Prolegomena zur Geschichte des Zeitbegriffs*, GA Band 20, Klostermann, Frankfurt

point in this is nothing other than a repetition of Plato's negative judgment of the Sophists, except for the fact that Plato continually enters into discussion with them, whereas Heidegger does not.

Why Heidegger remains silent on mimesis is rather enigmatic. Several reasons may be alleged, the most important of which is perhaps the opposition which guides Heidegger's thought – between real and unreal, proper and improper, original and non-original, and in which the real, the proper and the original are given priority without comment. Thus, there is talk of proper thought as opposed to improper thought, which is metaphysical and calculating [*das rechnende Denken*], and of an original word as opposed to the 'idle talk' which is only the repetition of what has already been said, of a true proximity of things as opposed to a thoughtless passing of all that is, and of the not yet technically controlled world as opposed to a world which may possibly come to ruin through technology. The tendency to understand history as deterioration, decline and alienation from the origin[82] and a certain nostalgia for the own, the proper, the original and pure, are undeniably present in Heidegger, as Derrida has remarked.[83] No doubt this

a.M. 1979, pp. 376-377 [*History of the Concept of Time. Prolegomena*, translated by T. Kisiel. Indiana University Press, Bloomington, IN, 1992, pp. 272-273.].

82. S. IJsseling, 'Sprache und Schrift', in: *Philosophie und Poesie*. Otto Pöggeler zum 60. Geburtstag. Band 2. Herausgegeben von A. Gethmann-Siefert. Frommann-Holzboog, Stuttgart 1988, pp. 105-124.

83. J. Derrida, 'Les fins de l'homme', in *Marges de la philosophie*, pp. 131-164 ['The Ends of Man', in *Margins of Philosophy*, pp. 109-136].

stands in the way of a radical reflection on the mimetic.

In addition to the foregoing, two things must be noted. In the first place, the relation between real and unreal, proper and improper, original and non-original in Heidegger is extremely complex. And secondly, this relation is in fact a mimetic relation which, it is true, is never referred to as such by Heidegger, but which is indeed operative and understood in a certain (to some extent Platonic) way by him. Lacoue-Labarthe writes: 'The refusal of Heidegger to take the concept of mimesis seriously is constant, but it seems ever more difficult to me not to see that in Heidegger's thought there is a fundamental mimetology at work.'[84]

In order to realize some of the complexity of the relation between the proper and the improper and the original and non-original, one must keep in mind that the proper is always already affected by the improper, that the origin is always already lost, that the (other) beginning is not behind us but ahead of us and that every appropriation (*Ereignis*) is always attended by an expropriation (*Enteignung*). Thus, the *Schritt zurück* of which Heidegger so frequently speaks is not a return to an original and not yet infected past, but an introspection into that which is, and the retrieval (*Wiederholung*) of the history of European philosophy is not a repetition of the already known, nor is it a Hegelian appropriation or recollection of the already thought, but is an attempt to liberate the possibilities – forgotten and blocked by the tradition – of what was once original, thus to turn them into possibilities once again. The original for Heidegger

---

84. Ph. Lacoue-Labarthe, *Imitations des Modernes*, p. 170.

is situated not in the past but in a future (*Zukunft*) which, so far as man is accessible to it, can come toward him.

With regard to the original, creative and edifying word of the poet, Heidegger remarks that as soon as it is said, it is essentially exposed to the possibility of repetition and thereby to deterioration and decline.[85] No speech can avoid this repetition in which a same word is said again and yet in which this repetition insures that no word is ever the same twice. Heidegger calls this the *Unwesen* of language, a decline of speech which can never be avoided.[86] All original saying, which is also always an origin of new words, is necessarily delivered up to its opposite – i.e., to repetition or reproduction, in which the origin is lost and withdraws. Therefore, for Heidegger, citing Hölderlin, language is '*der Güter Gefährlichstes*', the most dangerous of goods.[87]

Heidegger's talk here of an *Unwesen* and *Verfall* of language shows once more that there is at work in his thought a mimetology reminiscent of Plato. For Plato, too, no repeating (citing and reciting) is true speaking but make believe, a sham and imitation of true speaking. However, in contrast with Plato, Heidegger will contend that the original word is the word of the poet, and that the *Unwesen* of language belongs to the essence of language itself. According to Heidegger, inauthenticity is inherent to authenticity, and true speech is not speaking in one's own name such that the speaker has full insight into what he says and does and considers himself fully

---

85. M. Heidegger, 'Hölderlins Hymnen "Germanien" und "Der Rhein"' GA Band 30. Klostermann, Frankfurt a.M. 1980, p. 63.
86. *ibid.*, p. 64.
87. *ibid.*, p. 60.

responsible for his words, but is only that speech which answers to a more original word and which truly shows something.

The mimetology at work in Heidegger's thought does indeed exhibit all sorts of Platonic traits. In the light of a radical reflection on mimesis, several aspects of that thought could in fact be opened up for discussion. Among these would be his conception of history, his oppositions – functioning in the background – between the authentic and inauthentic and between the original and non-original, his covert homesickness for a real proximity and his search for a word which could truly name being [*Sein*]. At the same time, Heidegger also supplies us with some tools and opens the way for re-thinking mimesis in a non-metaphysical and non-Platonic way.[88] Although he does not speak explicitly of mimesis, it is still partly thanks to him that mimesis occupies a privileged position for the philosophers of difference. For that matter, in the foregoing, we, too, have been inspired by Heidegger.

The possibility of opening mimesis to discussion in a new way with the help of Heidegger can be found, for instance, in his thoughts on the work of art, on language, *logos*, *doxa* and, of course, on difference and *alètheia*. Yet, one could just as easily say that these central themes of Heidegger's thought are cast in a new light by the problem of mimesis. It is not our intention here to enter

---

88. 'Mimesis can be rethought and reinscribed within Heidegger's poetics.' J. Sallis, 'Heidegger's Poetics. The Question of Mimesis', in *Kunst und Technik*. Gedächtnisschrift zum 100. Geburtstag von Martin Heidegger. Herausgegeben von W. Biemel und F.W. von Hermann. Klosterman, Frankfurt a.M. 1989, p. 188.

elaborately into these issues. A few main features will suffice.

For Heidegger, the work of art is not an imitation or a depiction of reality, but a 'putting into operation of the truth.'[89] The essence of the image is not to be a representation, but to let be seen, to show.[90] Poetry is not a rendering, but a *Wieder-gabe*, a giving-back, which is understood as a *Frei-gabe*, an *Eröffnen*, a creating of an openness, and an *Einräumen*, a filling-up of space.[91] And this, then, is an openness and a space where gods and people, heaven and earth can appear. When there is talk of a 'putting into operation of the truth', it concerns truth as *alètheia*, understood as *Entbergung* and *Verbergung*, revealing and concealing. In the work of art (architecture, the visual arts and literature) something comes to light, something becomes visible, but, too, something withdraws and conceals itself.

The word, for Heidegger, is not a sign (*Zeichen*); the essence of speaking can not be understood from the character of words as signifying.[92] Saying is showing (*Zeigen*). Heidegger even goes so far as to contend that

89. M. Heidegger, 'Der Ursprung des Kunstwerkes', in *Holzwege*, GA 5, pp. 7-68 ['The Origin of the Work of Art', in *Basic Writings*, pp. 149-187. The complete text of this essay does not appear here, but has been included in the expanded and revised edition of the *Basic Writings* which appeared in 1993].
90. 'Das Wesen des Bildes ist: etwas sehen zu lassen.' M. Heidegger, *Vorträge und Aufsätze*. Neske, Pfullingen 1954, p. 200.
91. E. Escoubas, *Imago Mundi*, pp. 83-95.
92. 'Das Wesen des Sagens bestimmt sich nicht aus dem Zeichencharakter der Wörter der Sprache.' M. Heidegger, *Was Heisst Denken?* Niemeyer, Tübingen 1954, p. 123 [*What is Called Thinking?*, translated by J. Glenn Gray. Harper and Row, New York 1968, p. 203].

the moment in which a word is no longer understood as a showing but as a sign is one of the most important moments in the history of truth and of being. For thenceforth, truth is understood as correspondence and being as being at hand. Originally, the word is not a sign of something which is already there, but brings it about that something can appear as something. Heidegger writes: 'It is in words, in language that things first become and are.'[93] and 'if our essence would not stand in the power of language, every being would be inaccessible to us, the being which we ourselves are and the being which we are not.'[94] In (true) speech, something is shown and a certain clarity emerges, but at the same time in this showing and in this clarity something withdraws and conceals itself. 'Language is the lighting-concealing advent of Being itself', it says in the 'Letter on Humanism'.[95]

One could cite many other texts of Heidegger in this same line. With his thoughts on language, he moves into

---

93. 'Im Wort, in der Sprache, werden und sind erst die Dinge.' M. Heidegger, *Einführung in die Metaphysik*. Niemeyer, Tübingen 1953, p. 11 [*An Introduction to Metaphysics*, p. 13].

94. 'Selbst wenn wir tausend Augen und tausend Ohren, tausend Hände und viele andere Sinne und Organe hätten, stünde unser Wesen nicht in der Macht der Sprache, dann bliebe uns alles Seiende verschlossen: das Seiende, das wir selbst sind, nicht minder als das Seiende, das wir selbst nicht sind.' *ibid.*, p. 63 ['Even if we had a thousand eyes and a thousand ears, a thousand hands and many other senses and organs, if our essence did not include the power of language, all essents would be closed to us, the essent that we ourselves are, no less than the essent that we are not.' In *An Introduction to Metaphysics*, p. 82].

95. 'Sprache ist lichtend-verbergende Ankunft des Seins selbst.' M. Heidegger, *Brief über den Humanismus*, GA 9, p. 326 ['Letter on Humanism', in *Basic Writings*, p.206].

proximity with the Sophists, particularly Gorgias – an observation which is certainly not meant critically here. Heidegger would probably never admit to this, and perhaps there is a fundamental difference at stake. For Gorgias, as we have seen, the word is not a sign, but a powerful and dangerous instrument which can bring about a certain effect – namely, that man and thing appear as they appear, which is inevitably attended by a certain blinding. Like a true rhetorician, he assumes that one can control and master language, and on that basis possess an enormous and alarming power. Heidegger would subscribe to the view of language as powerful and dangerous, but not to the idea that one can control it. For him, language is always more powerful than man.[96]

Heidegger comes even closer to the Sophists and thereby to a non-Platonic position with his conception of appearance and *doxa*. In the chapter in his *Introduction to Metaphysics* which deals with being and appearance, it is explicitly stated that appearance belongs to being itself and that the separation of the two (in Plato) is one of the moments in which metaphysical thought is born.[97] According to Heidegger, the following belong to the domain of appearance: shining, beaming, gleaming, glowing, sparkling, showing off, distinguishing oneself, emerging, occurring, manifesting oneself, the face (in the sense of 'in the face of' or 'in the immediate presence of'), making one's appearance, phenomena, radiance and semblance

---

96. M. Heidegger, *Unterwegs zur Sprache*, Neske, Pfüllingen 1959, p. 124 [*On the Way to Language*, translated by P. Hertz. Harper and Row, New York 1971, p.].

97. M. Heidegger, *Einführung in die Metaphysik*, pp. 75-88 [*An Introduction to Metaphysics*, pp. 98-115].

in the sense of *mere* semblance and the 'as if'. For him, being and appearing are not opposed to one another but essentially belong together. The same is said of *doxa* and *alètheia*.

Heidegger distinguishes four meanings of *doxa*: 1. regard, in the sense of fame, renown, being famous, which is an effect of naming and praising; 2. to look like or appear as; 3. to only *look* like this or that, but to be different in fact; 4. an opinion formed on the basis of what seems to be like this or that.[98] Indeed, it is not certain these four registered meanings are the only ones. And perhaps it is better here to speak of dissemination than of polysemy. Heidegger speaks of *Vieldeutigkeit*, or 'plurivocity', and he adds that this is not a defect or negligence on the part of language, but the condition for great wisdom – for thus are the different traits of being [*Sein*] saved in this word.

According to Heidegger, appearance and being belong together inseparably, if only because appearance still *is* something, and speaking of something which somehow 'is' and yet falls outside the realm of being is nonsensical. When they are opposed, being is conceived of as being at hand, or as so-called 'real' existence. This implies that by far most of what concerns, interests or disturbs us would *not* be real – including that very interest or disturbance. Even if they are make-believe or mere imitation of others, this make-believe and this imitation are nonetheless part of who we really are. Still, the belonging-together of being and appearance does of course imply an ambivalence or, better, a polyvalence for being itself. To

---

98. *ibid.*, pp. 79-80 [pp. 102-103].

have seen this represents one of the most fundamental insights of Heidegger. What in his work is called the question of being is the question of this polyvalence.

What Heidegger says about *doxa* and *appearance* comes close to what we have said about mimesis in all its different manifestations. In short, *doxa* and appearance are interwoven with and always an effect of one or another form of mimesis. He comes a step closer to the problem of mimesis when he appeals to the *enargeia* to clarify what he means by *Lichtung des Seins* – or 'lighting of Being'.[99] *Enargeia* (not to be confused with *energeia*) means something like splendor, to shine, to excel, to be brilliant or striking. The word is cognate in the Greek *argos*, which means shiny white, or glittering; the stem of the word returns in the Latin word *argentum* (silver). *Enargeia* is a basic concept in the rhetorical tradition. It is regarded as an effect of mimesis.[100] The following is then at stake here: A good speaker (narrator, writer) knows how to render events and situations, persons and their adventures in such a way that the listener (reader) has the sensation of being himself present to it all as an eye witness. In and through the narration (*narratio*) – and this, of course, is a form of mimesis – the events, situations and persons appear in a clear, concrete, striking and possibly splendid way. They appear, however, where they are not – that is to say, not in the story. Quintilian

---

99. M. Heidegger, 'Das Ende der Philosophie und die Aufgabe des Denkens', in *Zur Sache des Denkens*, Niemeyer, Tübingen 1969, pp. 73ff. ['The End of Philosophy and the Task of Thinking', in *Basic Writings*, pp. 384ff.].
100. H. Lausberg, *Handbuch der literarischen Rhetorik*. Hueber, München 1973², §810.

speaks here of *evidentia in narratione*.[101] In a sense, in narrating (explaining, rendering) a displacement of so-called reality takes place. It appears in another place at another moment – namely, in that of the rendering, precisely through which it can appear. For understandable reasons, the art of speaking and writing in a way that makes this take place is thought highly of in literary and rhetorical tradition. It is a culminating point in mimetic art.

Heidegger remains silent as always about this rhetorical and mimetic aspect. Instead, he speaks of the *Lichtung des Seins* and about Cicero's translation of *enargeia* as *evidentia* – two matters which for him are not separable.

According to Heidegger, the word *enargeia* points at the phenomenon that sometimes sparkles, gleams, shines, or appears in itself and of its own accord. And, he adds, in order for something to sparkle and shine, there must first be a more original openness in which something can do so. This openness is called *Lichtung des Seins*. Heeding all the reserve and caution that this calls for, one perhaps could say that this *Lichtung* is a name for that which takes place in mimesis in all its different forms. The same might be said of *alètheia* as revealing and concealing, and of the *Ereignis* [appropriation] which is also *Enteignis* [expropriation]. Heidegger would object to such an interpretation on the grounds of what remains a Platonic conception of mimesis. However, it is clearly possible to interpret mimesis differently than did Plato or the Platonists. When mimesis is understood otherwise not

---

101. C. Ginzburg, 'Ekphrasis and Quotation', in *Tijdschrift voor Filosofie*, 50(1988), pp. 3-19.

from degrees of perfect correspondence, but instead from the distinction (*Differenz*) made above, from the displacement and the appearance of being where it is not, new light is shed on what Heidegger might mean by *Lichtung des Seins* and *alètheia*. Also important here are words such as *logos* (understood as exposition and gathering into a unity), *Austrag* (dissemination, unfolding), *Riss* (tear, notch) and *Zwiefalt* (twofold), all of which Heidegger uses to bring out the event of being. In addition to this, it may be said that a radical reflection on mimesis in the light of the rhetorical tradition problematizes speaking of an original presence, a real proximity and a true word that could say being.

In the above cited passage about *enargeia*, Heidegger remarks that Cicero translates this word as *evidentia*, thereby in fact giving it another meaning.[102] This is only one of many such remarks that he makes with regard to the translation into Latin of words including *alètheia*, *logos*, *physis*, *dikè*, *ousia*, *hypokeimenon* and *pseudos*, whereby it is always said to be an *Umdeutung* (different explanation), a *Verstellung* and a *Verdeckung*. Heidegger elaborates on this in his 1942-1943 lectures on Parmenides.[103]

Translating is a hermeneutic activity as well as a mimetic one. Before entering into this directly, it is important to recall a few general principles with respect to translating as it is conceived of by Heidegger. For Heidegger, translating is not simply a matter of language.

---

102. [For 'giving it another meaning', IJsseling uses the Dutch 'omduiden', which resonates with the German 'umdeuten', which in turn means 'to give another meaning.']

103. M. Heidegger, *Parmenides*, GA Band 54, Klostermann, Frankfurt a.M. 1982.

Words are not only translated, but are also transposed (*übersetzt* and *übergesetzt*) to another context, to another world. Thus, Greek words are transposed into a Roman world and, according to Heidegger, therefore to an imperial, curial and ultimately Romanic or Roman Catholic world. Then he makes a sharp but not very clear distinction between translating Greek words into the Roman or Romanic world and translating them into the Germanic world. For Heidegger, the translation from Greek into Latin – the romanization of the Greeks – is attended by 'a changing of the essence of truth and of being', and this is 'the proper event in history.'[104] In this context, he says 'Being initially occurs in language.'[105] In and through translating, the event of being takes place. This event is essentially characterized by disclosure and concealment.[106]

We observed that translating is a hermeneutic and mimetic operation. It is hermeneutic in the twofold meaning of the Greek *hermeneia*. First, this means to voice, to say in language. Aristotle's *Peri Hermeneias* (*de interpretatione, de enunciatione*) treats of this. It also means to interpret that which has already been voiced, that is: to

---

104. 'Das Entscheidende bleibt, dass die Romaniserung im Wesenhaften des griechisch-römischen Geschichtsbereichs angreift als ein *Wandel des Wesens der Wahrheit und des Seins* (Heidegger's italics). Dieser Wandel hat das Auszeichnende, dass er im Verborgenen bleibt und dennoch alles zum Voraus bestimmt. Dieser Wandel des Wesens der Wahrheit und des Seins ist das eigentliche Ereignis in der Geschichte.' M. Heidegger, *Parmenides*, GA Band 54, p. 66.
105. 'Das Sein gibt sich anfänglich ins Wort.' *ibid.*, p. 113.
106. 'Entbergung und Verbegung sind ein Grundzug des Seins.' *Ibid.*, p. 105.

say in other words and possibly in another language. Translating is also mimetic in a twofold sense. One of the many forms of mimesis is rendering events and acts in words. This is addressed in Aristotle's *Poetics*, a work concerned with the epic and the tragedy, which exist first and foremost in the rendering in words of possible and probable events. Further, mimesis also means a repeating of what has already been rendered in words. Such a repetition may take the form of citing and reciting (on stage, for example), but also of saying the same in a different way. In the latter case, *variatio* and *aemulatio* play an important part. Translating is saying the same in other words, in another way.

Though Heidegger frequently enters into the hermeneutic aspect of translating, he nonetheless remains, as always, silent with regard to the mimetic. Concerning translation as a hermeneutic activity he has made many important remarks, each of which require detailed analysis. However, in those remarks there is also an implicit mimetology at work. For Heidegger, translating is to transpose the same onto a different level. In the translation of Greek into Latin, this always seems to be a lower level. Here, again, the Platonic conception of mimesis plays a role. A reflection on mimesis from an Aristotelian or rhetorical perspective could shed a different light on what here is called transposition and a different level. Thereby, the 'change in the essence of truth and being' – meaning the history of being – might also be understood in a new way.

A current objection raised against Heidegger's thought boils down to the belief that for him there is no longer a criterion for truth. When being is appearance, truth unconcealedness and language the shiningly concealing arrival of being and the 'ursprüngliche Aufklingen der Wahrheit einer Welt' [original resonance of the truth of a world],[107] how can there still be any question of truth and untruth in the traditional senses of those words? According to Heidegger, it is indeed the case that we are without any criterion by which to measure that which appears by something else. But there is still the domain of the 'rightness' (*Richtigkeit*) of our statements. And these, of course, can be verified or falsified. Yet for Heidegger rightness versus wrongness and verification versus falsification suppose a more original dimension – the surprising fact that there is even something to be seen and said, something to be done and judged, unconcealedness. It is on this level that Heidegger's thought abides. Should one wish to raise the question of mimesis in a fundamental way, then one will have to concern oneself with such a level.

The traditional objection to Heidegger can also be raised against an interpretation of mimesis in which it is allotted a role of such importance as it has received in the foregoing. Does such an interpretation still leave room for a criterion by which to distinguish real and unreal? No doubt there is a level at which certain forms of counterfeit, forgery, make believe, deceit and show can be exposed for what they are. No one will contest this. On a more fundamental level, however, matters become extremely complicated. It then becomes far more difficult to draw clear lines between real and unreal, original and non-original, imaginary and non-imaginary, illusory and

---

107. M. Heidegger, *Nietzsche* I, p. 364 [*Nietzsche*, vol. II, translated by D.F. Krell. Harper and Row, New York 1984, p. 105].

non-illusory, and between products of the imagination and hard facts. To give a concrete example: do Antigone and Emma Bovary really exist or not? In any event, they exist as personages in a story, they are part of our world and play an important role in our culture. Does this concern original stories or already existing ones which are told again and in a different way? Are the expectations and suffering of Antigone and Bovary imaginary? And what about us? Aren't we ourselves personages in a network of stories told by others and by ourselves, preceding our birth and outlasting our death, opening and limiting the space in which we can be present to ourselves and to others? Our expectations and frustrations, our ideas and our identity, which we derive from others on the basis of mimetic relations – are they mere illusions? The mirror image – is it real? And what about the countless images which are held out to us and which determine how we see ourselves and reality? Is Michelangelo's representation of the final judgment – in the Sistine Chapel – less real than the final judgment which has not (yet) taken place? And is his David less real than the (legendary) shepherd's boy from Bethlehem? Are his paintings and statues less original than those of his predecessors which he tries to imitate and to excel in many respects? And when we see these paintings and statues, and are not only struck by their beauty – indeed, what is that? – but ourselves form an image of what it is to be human – is that mere fancy? And what about the images we are able to see in the cinema and on television? What about the numbers, ideas and ideal objects of which the sciences speak, and the innumerable products imitated and reproduced in our technical world?

Of course, one could make all sorts of distinctions here

– distinctions on which the whole history of thought has been spent. But in each such distinction new problems arise. What is called 'reality' shifts and displaces itself onto another level each time. It seems beyond question that all of the above examples involve meanings produced on the basis of mimesis. What we just referred to as displacement and transposition belong to what takes place in every form of mimesis. Mimesis *is* displacement, transposition to another level of reality – without that new level necessarily being either higher or lower than the first one. It is on the basis of displacement – which is thus appearance in another place and at another moment – that meanings can come into being. Accordingly, mimesis seems to be a sort of transcendental dimension, be it perhaps quasi- or simili-transcendental.[108] Consequently, a reflection on mimesis is a reflection not only on art and literature, theater and the mirror, reading and writing, but also on what we say when we use the word 'reality'.

Is mimesis the last word, then? Perhaps not. There is also the realm referred to as the 'ethical'. Now, it is a fact that many problems ranged under this heading are of a mimetic nature as well. People act as others do, and they judge these actions as others judge them. Ethical greatness usually consists in following an exemplary way of life, and even crime is usually far from original. To lead a moral life is to comply with the prevailing, and possibly reasonably justified manners, customs, ideals and obligations. This greatness and baseness and these rights and

---

108. The expression quasi- or simili-transcendental is derived from J. Derrida. Cf., for example, *Psyche*, p. 641. However, the term was in fact coined by Rodolphe Gasché.

duties can be thematized in art, literature and philosophy. But there is something further. Not only do people speak of reality and the course of events in the world, about others and about themselves, they also speak to and are spoken to by one another. Here, too, mimesis plays a part. Otherwise, people would not know how to do this and would not understand each other. Still, in this being spoken to and speaking to there is a dimension which does not belong to what appears. It is something which is neither of the order of the image or rendering, nor of the order of identity and doubling.[109] Thus, it can not be thematized. There are no words for it. However, it is supposed in all thematizing and in every word, for thematizing and speaking are always also a speaking to and a being spoken to. It falls 'outside' the domain of art and literature, and also of philosophy, though it takes place in every form of art and philosophy. Plato had a name for it: the idea of the Good, goodness, which, according to him, is of another order than that of being or, as Emmanuel Levinas puts it, *Otherwise than Being or Beyond Essence*. It is not impossible that this 'goodness' is the *ultimate* spring of every form of mimesis.

---

109. Cf. Th. de Boer, *Tussen filosofie en profetie. De wijsbegeerte van Emmanuel Levinas*. Ambo, Baarn, The Netherlands, 1988², pp. 40-42.